Define Your Voice

Narrowing Down Your Target Market

By Altovise Pelzer

Unless otherwise indicated, all scripture quotations are taken from the New Living Translation (NLT) version of the Bible

Define Your Voice

Table of Contents

Future

Continue to Learn

Stay Focused

Make Connections

Meet the Author

Past

"Like an eagle with wings outstretched, your voice, once you find it and use it, will allow you to soar."

Your voice is unique to you!

How many of us can remember when we
would be outside playing with our friends
and our mom or gmom (short for
grandmother) would stick their head out the
door and yell for us? Oh, don't act like I was
the only one! Everyone turned and looked at
you while you ran towards your house
mumbling under your breath about the
curlers in your mom's hair. Don't even think
about not stopping whatever you were doing
to find out what they wanted either. The
point is that we knew their voice and by the
tone of their voice we could often tell,

accompanied by the laughter of our friends, if we were in trouble for something. They had a unique voice.

Although technology has boomed with ideas and apps as far as the eye can see there is still one thing that remains the same...............there is power in the use of words! That can also be translated into there being power in the use of your voice. When I use the word voice in this book I am referring to your unique story. That would be that one thing that you overcame, that sickness that you were healed from or that abusive relationship that you came out of.

Your voice is the lesson learned along with the bumps and bruises that you gained during the fight. Your unique voice makes you relatable to a specific target audience and they are waiting for you to open your mouth.

This book will show you how to catch the attention of your target audience by pinpointing your unique voice. Transparency is necessary in today's world. The gaming industry, television, social media and movie trends show a rapidly growing desire for what is real. From childhood movies being remade into live-action movies to video games becoming more violent, there is a thirst for transparency.

How does this relate to your unique voice? Today, more and more people have become disengaged with the celebrity, artist, public speaker or coach who stands before people simply sharing their accolades. Where you are financially does not make you as great as knowing where you are mentally, emotionally and spiritually. Simply put, people are waiting for you to create a roadmap for them to get over the mountain, through the valley and across oceans. They want you, "Flaws and All" as Beyonce says.

Step by step we will take a look at you, the reader, from a perspective that you may not have thought about. Before today, you may not have had anyone tell you that you are powerful. We can count on our fingers and toes the people who have told us that we can't. As you go through this process, yes it is a process, you will gain a better understanding of who you are as an individual.

Let's begin with a few thought provoking

questions.

1. What has brought you to making the decision to be an entrepreneur?

_____

_____

_____

_____

_____

_____

_____

_____

_____

_____

_____

_____

2. What will this change do for you? For your family? For your relationships?

_____

_____

_____

_____

_____

_____

_____

_____

_____

_____

_____

_____

_____

_____

3. On a scale of 1 to 10, with 10 being 100% open to doing what it takes, how much are you willing to invest when it comes to your business.

_____

_____

_____

_____

_____

_____

_____

_____

_____

_____

_____

_____

_____

Be Bold

Be bold they say..................... For far too long people have intertwined being bold with being loud! While, that is one word that may define the voice of that individual at that moment, there is a better definition that we will utilize in this book.

Bold – showing an ability to take risks; confident and courageous

We can begin the book with being bold because it is a bold statement when you share what is in your heart. By talking about it you're accepting the healing process and choosing to share that process and the results with someone else. Don't you think that's kind of bold? No? How about using your boldness to create and change a life or even a city? There are those who are waiting for your bold action in order for them to move forward.

What does being bold look like for me?

Can we be honest? No two people are alike. Situations will vary by person because of perception. I don't want you to look at my journey and assume that yours is supposed

look anything like it. For me being bold
meant speaking out about being molested as
a child. It meant sharing what I endured
after finding out that my girls were
molested. I stepped out and created a book
series as part of my boldness. My unique
voice connects with women who have
endured abuse, molestation and rape who
now believe that they have no voice. They
are not the only people that my voice travels
to but we will talk about that later in the
book.

From the moments in my life when I cried
the most, I am able to help other women

realize their possibilities. That was not an easy journey. My first book took eight years before I completed and published it.

Yup...........I was slacking. Oh I talked a good talk about publishing and speaking but transforming those words into action was a whole other thing. I couldn't do it. I wasn't able to sit down and focus just on typing. My fear and insecurities became shackles around my dream. Even giving myself deadlines didn't help move my vision forward. Here I am eight years later with a book published, speaking engagements beginning to fill up my calendar and opportunities for me to encourage others.

Next in my bold step is helping you to not take eight years to birth your own vision. I feel like I'm having a "Do as I say, not as I do" moment with you. You remember those scoldings from our family members? It covered everything from smoking to cussing. Mine will be more of an encouragement than a scolding. I'm sure all those who are visual will have the image of me pointing my finger at them through the remainder of the book. That's okay as long as you know that I am doing it out of love.

What does being bold look like for you?

I will sum up your boldness in as few words as possible...........You are bold! Lol. Is this statement easier to read than to digest? It used to be hard for me to digest as well. Me, the introvert, the shy person, the people pleaser and the "great friend", could never be as bold as they are. Have you said this same statement to yourself either out loud or in your own head?

To walk in your boldness first you will have to walk out of the titles, stereotypes and the perceptions that others have placed upon you. Don't you dare close this book! Yes there will be something we need to strip away from your personal self image. That's okay. I had to do the same thing. Next you will see a list of statements and questions that I want you to think about. I've even given you some space to write things down as you go through the process.

I want to Be Bold!

1. What is holding your back?

_____

_____

_____

_____

_____

_____

_____

_____

_____

_____

_____

_____

_____

_____

2. Is it something that can harm you physically,

mentally or emotionally?

_____

_____

_____

_____

_____

_____

_____

_____

_____

_____

_____

_____

_____

_____

3. How was this seed of fear planted into your life?

_____

_____

_____

_____

_____

_____

_____

_____

_____

_____

_____

_____

_____

_____

_____

4. Who has been the gardener taking care of this seed of fear?

_____

_____

_____

_____

_____

_____

_____

_____

_____

_____

_____

_____

_____

_____

_____

5 Write five affirmations about yourself and start them off by saying "I am Bold enough to.........."

_____

_____

_____

_____

_____

_____

_____

_____

_____

_____

_____

_____

_____

_____

Pivotal Moments

"There was a lesson in the moment when you closed your eyes and thought you couldn't bear it any longer, you're a conqueror!"

Turn here......................We hate when people who are giving us directions wait until the last minute to tell us when to turn. It creates a chain reaction of eye rolling and wanting to unlock the doors as you are driving. There are sometimes when life gives us that same last minute turn notification. Those pivotal can be when we fall if we are not careful.

Pivot - turn on or as if on a pivot.

Pivotal Moments are a game changer. The adrenaline is pumping, your eyes are glazed over from the tears and you struggle to breath! What happened? In this moment we cried more than we've ever cried before. We closed the blinds because the natural light burned our eyes. Questions swirled around our heads and time became a lump in your throat.

You were hit hard and it knocked you down, it changed the course of your life or made you run in the opposite direction. That was a pivotal moment. The hit that you received was a seed that opened and produced roots. Those roots affected your vision, your heart, your mind, and your actions and every part of your being. Do you get the visual?

When I was molested as a child, accompanied by not having my father around, the roots of that molestation affected all areas of my life. Low self esteem, how I thought I was supposed to act and react when it comes to love and what was or wasn't beautiful. I know now that this pivotal moment set me up tp be who I am today. The scars from that moment in my life became evident as I began to walk in being an individual.

Then it happened! The scabs were removed and it reopened the wounds. I found out that my girls were molested. What a blow to my self confidence. The new found perception I had worked so hard to created fell like a house of cards. What followed were moments that I can't even truly explain in words. I can almost relate it to being knocked out, being awakened and then being knocked out again.

Our moments may not have been the same but the process remains the same. Knocked down, skinned knees, bruised ribs, tears and then at some point we get up. For you getting up may have included getting a divorce, credit repair, buying a new house, or taking on a new job. For me, getting up meant moving to a different state, joining an amazing church family and becoming a better version of me.

My Pivotal Moments were a game changer!

1. Think of one of your pivotal moments.
What are three to five of the smaller steps
you took to move forward in that situation?

_____

_____

_____

_____

_____

_____

_____

_____

_____

_____

_____

_____

_____

_____

2. Look at those three to five smaller steps that you took. How did they affect you personally? Your family? Your business? Your relationships?

_____

_____

_____

_____

_____

_____

_____

_____

_____

_____

_____

_____

_____

3. What did you learn about people from these moments? (Actions, Emotions etc)

_____

_____

_____

_____

_____

_____

_____

_____

_____

_____

_____

_____

_____

4. Look back at your "Be Bold" statements that you created. Now I want you to take them one step further. "I am bold enough to _____ because I did _____ in the midst of my situation."

_____

_____

_____

_____

_____

_____

_____

_____

_____

_____

_____

_____

_____

5. Do you believe that other people have or will have a similar pivotal moment? If so, what did you learn that you can share to help them?

_____

_____

_____

_____

_____

_____

_____

_____

_____

_____

_____

_____

_____

_____

_____

_____

_____

_____

You are Strong

"Strength is the mindset of those willing to let go of control."

That moment when you have reached the finish line is a feeling like no other. People are cheering and crying because of the accomplishment you just made. Can I be honest? Sometimes we forget that there are small victories that led up to you crossing the finish line.

Strong - the quality or state of being strong, in particular

Who me? Yes you! Couldn't be! Then who? Some remember these words from the childhood song "Who Stole the Cookies From the Cookie Jar?" Yes, I took it way back with that one. When there were those who tried to blame things on us we are quick to defend ourselves. When people compliment us we often run to that same line of defense. Why is that?

For a large part of my life I did not know how to take a compliment. I would always highlight some negative flaw to dim the light that someone was trying to shine on me. So before I go into just how strong you are, I'll give you a list of the lines you will already be thinking. Don't you dare think about putting this book down either! This is apart of the process. Highlight the ones you were thinking.

- I deserved it
- I let it happen
- It ruined me
- I'm just me
- I'm no different than anyone else
- Others have done it better

- They said_____

- I didn't have my mother

- I didn't have my father

- I could have done better

- It was my fault

- Should have seen it coming

Take a moment to realize that those statements and thoughts we have about ourselves were created by it or them. It or them has planted a seed that affects your self esteem. It and them have become a life vest when they should have been a stepping stone. So I need you to cut that line right now. Say it loud..........Say it boldly.......Say it daily. It and them are my stepping stones not my life vest!! You have learned how to swim so let that life vest go.

Now we can dive into how strong you are. You are a bodybuilder even when that's not what you see in the mirror. How so? Well go back and look at your pivotal moments. You made it, you overcame, you were victorious and I know this because you are here. Not just here physically but here reading this book. You realize, even if it's only slightly, that what you went through is the link to your unique voice.

What you endured did not kill you. Like in 2 Corinthians 4:8-9, we can now see that God did not abandon us. In the midst our situation we often see few if any solutions. Yet here you are to tell the story. Remember when I started off by talking about what happens when we reach the finish line? Well I want you to start looking at the mile markers on the way to the finish line. You didn't go to jail, you didn't turn to drugs or if you did you fought to get free of it, you learned to love again, you learned to trust again, you learned to walk again, you put on your wig and slayed not only the ball but every event after that..............yea, you did that!

"It is the small accomplishments that guide you towards the finish line"

Motivational quotes are birthed out of the victories, trials and failures in a person's life. They become popular because they are relevant and transparent. This chapter has been about not just realizing that you are strong but seeing that your strength is what someone else is fighting to get. With that being said, you are going to create your own quotes.

My strength exceeds my expectation

1. Name three victories you have had in your life.

_____

_____

_____

_____

_____

_____

_____

_____

_____

_____

_____

_____

_____

_____

_____

2. How did you feel when you were in the process of getting that victory? What emotions did you display?

_____

_____

_____

_____

_____

_____

_____

_____

_____

_____

_____

_____

3. What were the actions and reactions that stand out the most in your mind when it comes to the process you went through to gain your victory?

_____

_____

_____

_____

_____

_____

_____

_____

_____

_____

_____

4. Using your responses from the second and third question, create a series of quotes. Use an emotion and an action or reaction.

_____

_____

_____

_____

_____

_____

_____

_____

_____

_____

_____

_____

5. It's time to test the theory and see if it's true.

I want you to post one of the quotes you

created. Then write the responses that you get.

_____

_____

_____

_____

_____

_____

_____

_____

_____

_____

_____

_____

Present

Be careful of your words, they can either

build you a bridge or a prison

Write the Vision

Here is where we get caught up because of technology. Yea, I said it. We've become so reliant on our phones that we miss the significance of a piece of paper and a pen. (Or pencil if that's what you prefer) Why is it so significant you ask?

1. A written goal brings clarity
2. A written goal or idea becomes reaffirmed
3. A written goal gives direction
4. A written goal allows us to get all the ideas out of our head to organize them

5. A written goal allows you to track progress

6. A written goal holds you accountable

There is also a biblical importance to writing things down.

1. The message will be carried on accurately

Then the LORD said to me, "Write my answer plainly on tablets, so that a runner can carry the correct message to others.   Habakuk 2:2

2. Things written down hold you accountable

[5] And the one sitting on the throne said, "Look, I am making everything new!" And then he said to me, "Write this down, for what I tell you is trustworthy and true."   Revelation 21:5

So do you get the importance of writing things down? When it comes to you the individual, the brand, the mother, the wife, the student and the teacher it will always be necessary that you write things down. If not, you will always be attempting to play catch up as bills, appointments and situations shift your current situation. No, we can't be prepared for everything but we can be prepared for something.

It is just as important to write down what is currently going on as it is to write down your goals. Don't get overwhelmed............ we don't have to start with the big things just yet. Let's start small. We are going to look at your pivotal moments again and come up with some goals for the next few days.

I want you to choose one pivotal moment that you want to focus on. For some this will be difficult because we tried so hard to bury what happened to us. We covered the scars with long sleeves and turtle necks believing that strangers walking by us could see beneath them. I have you just choosing one moment because I will show you how that one moment set you up for victory.

Did you pick one? Great. Let's get to writing.

1. During your pivotal moment, what are three things that helped you?

_____

_____

_____

_____

_____

_____

_____

_____

_____

_____

_____

_____

_____

_____

_____

_____

_____

2. How would your pivotal moment have changed if you knew these things before the moment happened?

_____

_____

_____

_____

_____

_____

_____

_____

_____

_____

_____

_____

_____

_____

_____

_____

3. What scars do you have from the experience?

_____

_____

_____

_____

_____

_____

_____

_____

_____

_____

_____

_____

_____

_____

4. Write out five to ten powerful statements about what the information you have can do for someone else. (ex. If someone would have told me the pan was hot, I wouldn't have burned myself.)

_____

_____

_____

_____

_____

_____

_____

_____

_____

_____

_____

_____

_____

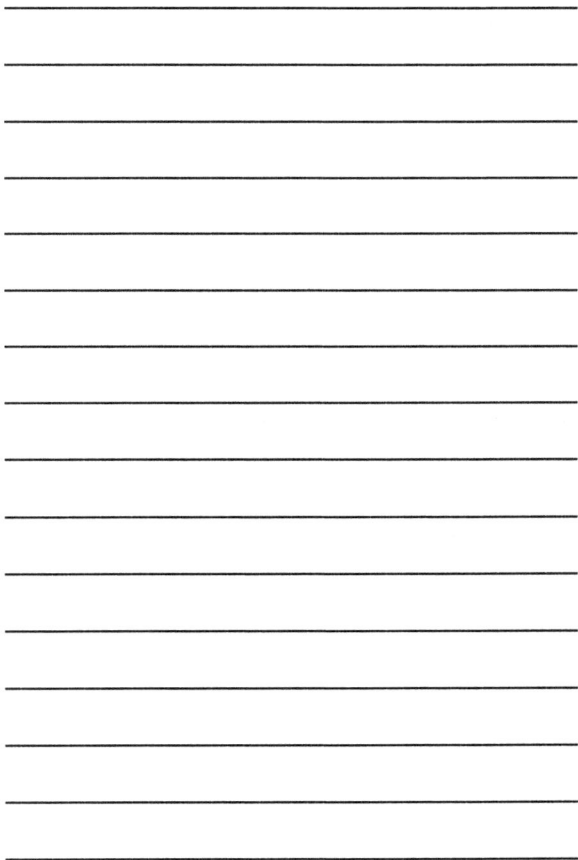

5. What are three ways you can share these tips?

_____

_____

_____

_____

_____

_____

_____

_____

_____

Change Your Words

In the previous chapter we created your vision. Yea, I know, you didn't even realize that it happened. Go ahead and look at it. You have your target audience, you have transparent experiences that you can share and you have a way to share it. Just like that. What's next is changing not only what we've been saying but how we say it.

People can become easily distracted or offended by the words of others but they can also become motivated and inspired by the words of others. I know this is a fact because I can recall times when I was easily offended by my perception of someone else's words or when I was motivated by someone else's words. I said in the beginning of the book that words have power. So, now it's time to tap into your power.

What you say?

Through the healing process we are no longer bound up by the by the pivotal moments of our past so there comes a time when we have to change our words to align with that. People in prison speak a certain way. There are phrases and slang that they use that people outside of jail do not understand. There is a certain way that we talk when were in the midst of pivotal moment. The jargon has to be translated so those who are reading what you wrote or are listening to what you are saying can understand.

How you say it!

Are you bitter or better? There is a huge difference and it will show up in how you talk about your pivotal moment. Are you speaking from a heart of forgiveness or hatred? Don't think you have to wear a mask or pretend to be anyone other than you. I need you to be authentic.

For me, being authentic means that you are able to share the pain and the purpose in your pivotal moment. People need both! There will be those who follow you even if you lean more to one side than the other. It's better to stay grounded by sharing the good, the bad and the ugly then to have people believing that there is only one side to a pivotal moment.

Power words create an emotional, mental and physical change when they are heard. They can create a bridge or a personal prison when it comes to sales, coaching, writing and public speaking. For example, words like "sale" are attention grabbing. People will walk into a store they had no intentions on going into simply because they saw the word sale in the window. It draws people to at least see what the "sale" is.

There are power words that will draw people into your world. Take the opportunity today, if you have not already realized it, to see that you are the expert. Your pivotal moment made you an expert and you have the scars to prove it. Walk in that title. The questions for this chapter will take some deep thought and may stir up some emotions that you buried. That's okay. There are others who have buried those same emotions and they need you to come with your shovel to help them dig them up.

Say it!

1. Think about the conversations that you have had with other people about your pivotal moment. What are five words that others have said that stand out? Why?

_____

_____

_____

_____

_____

_____

_____

_____

_____

2. What are five words that you have said about

your pivotal moment that stand out? Why?

_____

_____

_____

_____

_____

_____

_____

_____

_____

_____

_____

_____

3. Look up some synonyms and antonyms for

the ten words that you have.

_____

_____

_____

_____

_____

_____

_____

_____

_____

_____

_____

_____

_____

3. When reading these words what emotions do you feel? Can you remember who said them to you or just when it was said?

_____

_____

_____

_____

_____

_____

_____

_____

_____

_____

_____

4.I want you to create a tree. (yes this has turned into an art class. Lol) Your pivotal moment is the trunk and the ten words you've been working on are the roots. Don't put any leaves on the tree yet.

5. That tree is a powerful image right? Now add the leaves. The leaves are ways that you can use those words as well as your pivotal moment to change the world.

Take Action

We have definitely been on a journey. You've created a vision, created content and looked at ways to market, through words, to your target audience. Oh, we are not done just yet! By now you should know that I am not going to let you off that easy. It's time to take action!

Taking action will be something unique to you. It can range from starting a women's group to doing a weekly motivational class at your neighborhood school. This chapter will be short but the questions are meant to turn the fire up on everything you have written down.

Think big!!! It's time to step away from the security blanket. When people think of taking action they often teeter totter between big and little steps to reach their ultimate goal. Today we will take a big step that will seem little as we get closer to our ultimate goal. It's time to create a product or service.

Yes, creating a product or service is a big step. It sets you apart from others who have a similar story but remember we are already walking in the title of being an expert.

What will you create?

1. The things that you wrote about in the previous chapters are your personal experiences. Which of these experiences have happened or will happen to others? (Get the statistics)

_____

_____

_____

_____

_____

_____

_____

_____

2. What do people use as a resource before, during and after a pivotal moment like the ones you went through?

_____

_____

_____

_____

_____

_____

_____

_____

_____

_____

_____

3. What are the top three complaints from people who have a similar pivotal moment?

_____

_____

_____

_____

_____

_____

_____

_____

_____

_____

_____

_____

4. Out of the statistics, the complaints and resources that you found were missing or in low supply, I want you to choose one that you will start today. What is it? How will it help? Who needs it?

_____

_____

_____

_____

_____

_____

_____

_____

_____

_____

5. Out of the products and services that are already in large supply, I want you to choose three things you would choose to do differently.

_____

_____

_____

_____

_____

_____

_____

_____

_____

_____

6. What will you create? A product or a service? Only choose one. Write out as many details as you can about it.

_____

_____

_____

_____

_____

_____

_____

_____

_____

_____

_____

_____

The Future

"The impossible became doable when you

said yes, and completely possible when you

asked for help."

Continue to Learn

Look at how far you have come with the completion of each chapter. You've opened up doors of opportunities and experiences by saying that you were ready to tap into the greatness on the inside of you.

Through this book you either started a fire, added lighter fluid to make the fire bigger or uncovered the fire that was already blazing on the inside of you. That is a huge accomplishment. Don't let it stop here with this book. Set up a learning schedule for yourself by reading, listening to books on audio and joining classes. Even local libraries have free classes that you can do online.

When I say create a learning schedule, I mean set up a personal calendar of books you want to read or classes that you want to take in order to grow yourself, your business and your family. It can be anything from learning more about essential oils to taking a life certification class. Don't make a list of them; just write them on your calendar around holidays or major events

and appointments. (That's a trick I use)
Doctor's offices are a great place to read
and watch an instructional video.

Don't forget that you have to make time to
grow. Yes, our schedules are full with
husbands, children, relationships,
friendships, work and life but if your
purpose is as great as I know mine is then
making time is worth it.

Keep growing....

1. What are five ways that you can invest in your purpose? Be as specific as possible.

_____

_____

_____

_____

_____

_____

_____

_____

_____

_____

2. What have you invested in that did not yield a return in your life? How did it affect you?

_____

_____

_____

_____

_____

_____

_____

_____

_____

3. What are the things that you have sacrificed by NOT investing in your purpose? What are you willing to sacrifice to invest in your purpose? (Be specific)

_____

_____

_____

_____

_____

_____

_____

_____

_____

Get......and Stay Focused

You know how it is. We sit down to write and then we remember to take something out for dinner so we get up. When we get to the kitchen we see dishes in the sink so we start doing dishes. There is trash in the trash can so we take out the trash and when we go outside we notice that the car needs to be washed. Seven hours later we make it back to our computer or desk wondering where the time has gone.

Life and all its ups and downs will get you off track. Ooh look, a squirrel. Yes those infamous squirrel moments are real and they take away from our to-do list and zap our goals into oblivion.

Don't believe me? How many times have you put down this book? What was the reason you put down the book? How long did it take you to pick the book back up? What did you do in between the time you put down the book and picked it back up? This cycle repeats itself regularly.

So now we need to put some rules of engagement in place in order to give a priority to our goals. There will be times that we need to put out phones on do not disturb or turn off the television but first let's get clear about setting goals.

Learn to K.I.S.S. your goals and you will spend less time in your head. Sounds like a cure all right? It's true. K.I.S.S. stands for Keep It Simple Stupid. (We will say Sister instead of stupid) What is the goal and what are five steps to move me closer to that goal? Don't over complicate it. Think of the five steps as stepping stones because stepping stones are not meant for you to stand on for a long time. Stepping stones are meant for you to move forward and only be there momentarily.

Next we have to get clear about what distracts us. People, things and even time can be a distraction. Yes we are known for watching the clock when we have a deadline. We waste precious moments watching the second hand slowly move forward. Believe me, for someone who it took eight years to finish one book, I know all too well about what distracts us from

our greatness.

Fear was another big distraction for me. I

started and stopped many times even when

I had a deadline in place but it wasn't until I

looked at the truth about my fear that I

moved forward.

Let's get focused!

1. Think about the product or service that you are creating. How can you K.I.S.S. it? What five steps are you going to take to reach this goal?

_____

_____

_____

_____

_____

_____

_____

_____

2. What are the top five things that distract you when you have something to do? (Be as specific as possible)

_____

_____

_____

_____

_____

_____

_____

_____

_____

_____

3. What can you do to counteract these distractions in order to accomplish your K.I.S.S. goals?

_____

_____

_____

_____

_____

_____

_____

_____

_____

_____

4. Fear is a big distraction. What are the fears that you have about creating your product or service? We talked about fear being a seed. How was this seed of fear planted? Who planted it?

_____

_____

_____

_____

_____

_____

_____

_____

_____

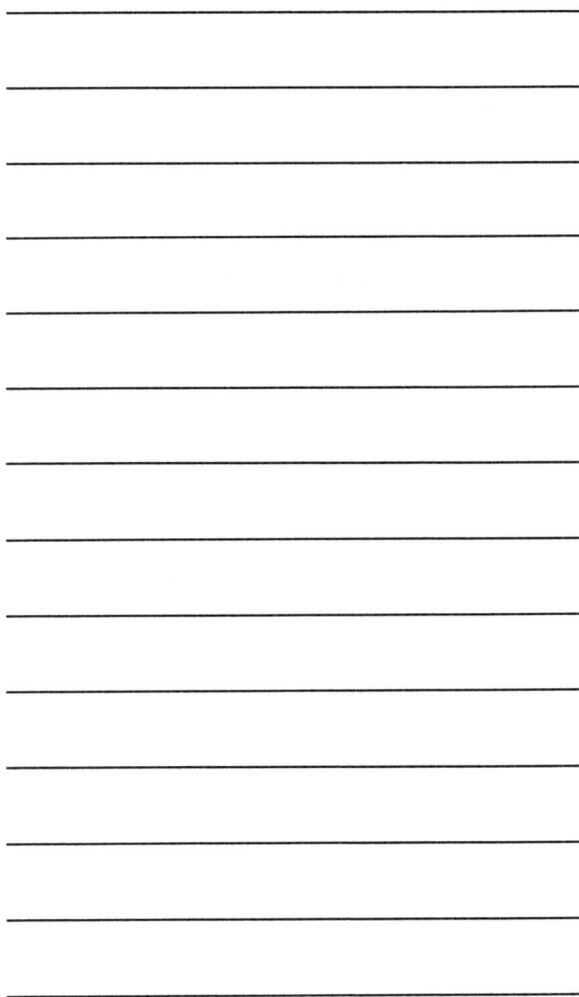

5. I want you to go back to your Be Bold statements that you created earlier in the book. You are going to add one last piece to it. "I am bold enough to _____ because I did _____ in the midst of my situation to cast out the fear of_____."

_____

_____

_____

_____

_____

_____

_____

_____

_____

_____

_____

6. Take the next five days to accomplish one step a day towards achieving your goal. Don't forget to K.I.S.S. it and each time you see a distraction or become fearful I want you to go back to your Be Bold statement.

Make Connections

You can see the finish line in the distance and you know you are almost there but then it happens. Your mind says keep pushing but your body seems to be slowing down. Just before you completely stop moving a hand suddenly is resting on your shoulder. Words break through the noise of your thoughts saying, "Come on, We got this!"

For some that was all you needed to hear to gain a sudden boost of adrenaline. "We got this" is a very powerful statement that can become a solid foundation. Yes you are great as an individual but there is power in numbers.

This chapter is all about networking. Yikes, I just felt you cringe. The world wishes for us to be an island unto ourselves because if we stand united and focused on a common goal we can accomplish so much more then we could alone. We often don't want to share our ideas and goals because we are afraid that someone will steal them or sabotage us.

First I need you to refocus your idea of networking.

Networking is not:

- An opportunity to be a copy cat
- An opportunity to be over the top with promoting ourselves (balance is key)
- An opportunity to network with people you already know

Networking is:

- An opportunity to grow yourself and your business through asking questions
- An opportunity to be your true self (No mask zone)
- An opportunity to perfect the elevator pitch
- An opportunity to create a time to follow up
- An opportunity to network with people you don't know

These are just a few of the dos and don'ts

Meet the Author

Altovise Pelzer, the author

of "The PRESS", a series of self-

help books for businesses,

women and families, is the CEO
of Define Your Voice Academy. Born
and raised in Philadelphia, PA,
Altovise was encouraged to write at
the age of eight by her grandmother
and she later found that developing a
love of writing would get her through
many difficult situations. What she
didn't know, was that writing would
also be a catalyst for her business, a
gateway to connecting with youth
and an opportunity to advocate for
those who feel as though they have

lost their voice.▯

Altovise is currently strengthening her passion of motivating women and youth through speaking, her holiday anti bullying youth initiative #GiftsForChange and in the pages of her first book series titled "The Press:Eight Stages of Pressing through difficult situations"▯She finds inspiration for her book series and conference topics from life experiences surrounding the molestation of her two daughters, fighting homelessness, the loss of her mother, learning to trust again and love. She encourages both women and youth to #KeepPRESSing no matter what circumstances they may find themselves in. .

Altovise is a mother, sister, mentor, friend, motivational coach and advocate. With so many hats, Altovise finds joy in spending time with her children and siblings doing

what she loves most which is simply

laughing.